T0142638

I Am Empowered
Freedom and Spirit of the Ride

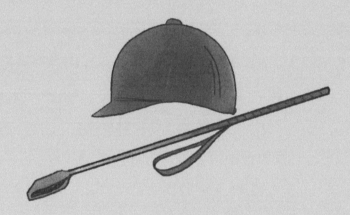

Written by Douglas Macauley

Illustrated by Valerie Bouthyette

Balboa Press books may be ordered through booksellers or by contacting:

Balboa Press
A Division of Hay House
1663 Liberty Drive
Bloomington, IN 47403
www.balboapress.com
844-682-1282

Interior Image Credit: Valerie Bouthyette

ISBN: 979-8-7652-4688-7 (sc)
ISBN: 979-8-7652-4689-4 (hc)
ISBN: 979-8-7652-4687-0 (e)

Library of Congress Control Number: 2023920872

Print information available on the last page.

Balboa Press rev. date: 11/21/2023

BALBOA.PRESS
A DIVISION OF HAY HOUSE

To my daughter, Madelyn,
who embodies this story about a girl
and her horse;

and to her dear cat, Lovey,
and all the amazing horses in my life
that teach me unconditional love.

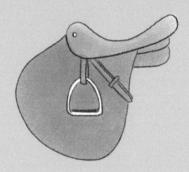

About the Book

In *I Am Empowered*, a teenage girl and her horse develop a deep and meaningful relationship on a journey through their adventures riding together. She learns empowerment while being in the flow with her horse as they embrace the ever-changing conditions that await them. Her regular visits to the equestrian center become an all-inclusive experience, and as her self-awareness expands, she builds a dynamic relationship with her horse while staying grounded and centered during her everyday life. This amazing journey creates joy in her life because she cares for her horse and connects with him on a deeper level.

About the Author

Douglas Macauley lives in Germantown, Maryland. He is a dedicated father with children spanning two generations: a daughter age fourteen, and a son age thirty-four. With degrees in electrical engineering and computer science, Douglas builds on his three decades as an electrical engineer for his work as a children's book author, mindfulness practitioner, life coach, and intuitive energy healer. His children's book series teaches empowerment through body awareness and mindfulness.

As I gently awaken, feeling the warmth and bright glow of the sunshine entering through the window, I absorb the energy of the sun as it creates an organic spark throughout my body. I take in a deep breath with excitement and anticipation of my day, knowing I will be riding my horse, Freedom.

Freedom awaits me as I begin to feel a deep connection with him. He knows I will arrive at the stable soon to greet him with an open heart and loving embrace. I take in another deep breath and exhale with ease as my nervous system relaxes, my mind surrenders, and my body feels in the flow so that I may arrive in the presence of Freedom with my energy balanced and grounded. He deserves to receive me in my finest energetic state, just as I deserve his balanced and grounded presence.

I am grateful for having Freedom in my life. His unconditional love and expanded heart are gifts to me that I feel deeply when we become one during our ride.

He teaches me that he is a mirror to me, yet he exemplifies his most amazing qualities when we are together.

I am blessed, for he is what makes my life so enhanced with profound joy.

Arriving at the stable, I pause and take in the multidimensional beauty of all the horses and feel their awareness of my presence. They each have their own unique and energetic state of being.

5

Horses are deeply grounded and have a strong connection with nature and humans, yet they continue to learn why they have chosen to experience this life with humans—it is a mutual teaching and learning relationship.

I approach the horses in a slow yet subtle manner while continuing to observe their awareness of my presence. The manner of my approach and conscious observation is a self-reflection that I am fully present in this moment as this honors myself and the horses. Self-reflection is part of my process in learning empowerment and the steps to becoming more mindful in my daily life. My awareness grows more every day and creates the space to appreciate all I have in my life, and this appreciation in turn strengthens the bonds I have with others.

These amazing horses are my teachers, and as I surrender to that greater knowing, I learn deeply because my mind is open, my body is relaxed, and I allow myself to surrender to the flow. All good things come from the flow, the stream of life from which all self-knowledge is birthed.

This deeper learning is a full body awareness and comprehension that does not come from the mind alone, for the mind interprets the physical intelligence of the body.

Each morning when I engage with my horses, I mindfully embrace these steps, which are essential before any ride. A fundamental, conscious energetic connection is inspired to happen as I create a safe container for both me and my horse. In taking these steps, I have set a foundation for the remainder of my day.

My horse and I become one, and this oneness creates our playful dance throughout the day as we teach each other not just the mechanics of riding but the freedom and spirit of the ride. Our symbiotic relationship continues to grow along with us.

I begin to feel deeply grounded in my own power and presence while noticing Freedom has slowly settled into a space that feels a bit safer. Initially, his nervous system felt scattered and tense, but he begins to relax, knowing I am there for him and with him.

Perhaps Freedom had a stir in the night that kept him on guard and created an energetic, overstimulated response upon my arrival, but these are ever-changing and simply part of his natural defense mechanisms.

It is important for animals and humans to feel safe; feeling grounded, centered, and empowered creates the basis for this safety.

I offer Freedom his morning meal and treat to start the day, then begin to groom him with a gentle touch and caring embrace. Freedom's nervous system relaxes more as he too stands in his power, knowing soon that we will ride together and be free to truly express ourselves, grounded in the joy that exists within us and between us.

As I mount Freedom bareback, his energy shifts once more as we adapt to each other with greater solidity.

Although we are individually grounded, we create a unified ground whereby energy radiates from our hearts and we become one.

Now we may move forward in a relaxed and flowing way, grounded in this flow as we move to stay still.

The beauty of the trees and surrounding forest invites us into an entirely new level of grounding, peace, and joy.

As we walk into the lush forest, Freedom's heart expands, and my heart begins to shift and clear the fragments of stress from everyday life that was held in my body.

Freedom begins to show me the path to this spirit of the ride. We continue to walk and to be bodily present as we are introduced into the amazing nature realm.

We breathe in the crisp morning air. As the oxygen moves through our bodies, it creates a light and spacious feeling, revitalizing all our cells.

Space is an important element for the flow and a more embodied feeling of being grounded.

The sun shimmers through the trees, and the subtlety of the wind envelopes us with more energy as we connect with the elements of nature.

The trees invite us to ground more deeply. We become more fully grounded with the earth—free-flowing like the wind, energized by the sun—and feel the fire in our hearts as we embark upon our journey.

My heart fills with love and passion. This is my path to continued freedom, joy, and empowerment while I get to honor myself in what I need for my well-being. Freedom teaches me extreme self-care as he embodies an unbridled state of being.

I begin to slow down on the trail and sink into a deeper level of connectedness with Freedom and nature. I feel the natural heartbeat of the forest as it soothes my nervous system. My breath becomes relaxed as the lower part of my body connects much more with Freedom. His awareness expands, his loving heart energy grows, and our heartbeats become one with the earth.

Creating our foundation with all that is, I know we are all connected yet safe and empowered on our journey through life.

When we balance our individuality and our compassion for others, we can move through life with greater fulfillment.

Freedom leads me through the forest, and I begin to transition into a trot. Synchronized fluidly, we glide with much ease as the air sweeps beneath us to give us the energetic lift that fills our existence.

The excitement mounts as I feel the lightness and agility of moving in any direction, which feeds my spirit. At any turn, I know and feel deeply that my intent is to stay grounded and connected with the earth and that I have the strength to navigate a safe and prosperous journey.

Out of the corner of my eye, I see a deer darting through the woods in a frantic and scattered pattern. I assume he is the father of the fawn I see nearby, alert to the intruder who has compromised their safety and become a possible predator in the woods.

Freedom begins to shudder and is thrown off-center. My energy shifts to a state of concern. The compromised energetic connection with Freedom doesn't feel supportive and becomes a bit frightening for me as well. My senses and his senses become challenged, and our nervous systems grow in heightened alert.

In all the intensity it is experiencing, my body begins to remember the foundational components necessary for stability and feeling safe.

I begin to use my conscious breath to move the energy of chaos through me to relax my nervous system. As I begin to self-regulate, my flowing breath becomes accompanied by an automatic energetic pull to the earth.

My body energetically affirms these foundational components as I regain my sense of feeling deeply grounded.

Once I equalize these energies in my body, Freedom and I greet each other with a mutual feeling of safety and of being grounded once again. We each have reset our nervous systems in our own processes yet come together after we individually return to equilibrium.

In a momentary reflection, after the somewhat startling experience of encountering the frightened deer and his fawn, we reduce our trot to a walk so that we may honor ourselves returning to this natural energetic state.

This is our birthright for being empowered and free to choose the path that brings us the most joy in life. I realize the deer and the fawn energetically showed us how they went into a flight response, after which their nervous systems recovered with the capacity to return to normalcy by simply shaking off the anxious energy that had momentarily built up in their nervous systems.

Deer have a nervous system similar to that of humans, but humans have a tendency to hold unwanted energy that may be consistent with fear in the body and mind. This energy has the potential to compound unless we attend to it and consciously choose to release it.

Much to my surprise, in my recovery process, this experience has allowed me to settle more deeply into a sense of confidence and awareness. I am always safe, even during challenges that arise, because when I choose to stay true to my passion, it sparks my entire body and being.

I am rewarded with more gifts to secure my body, an everlasting and growing sense of connectedness with everything and everyone. I am free to choose my path and grow my inner strength through these experiences. It is my birthright.

Freedom and I have grown together in this experience and have become more connected as we absorb all we have been gifted in learning. Our bodies as a whole learned to become more present through this process, and as a result we have grown much more grounded, knowing and feeling we worked through it together.

I feel a much greater untethered strength and confidence to see a greater forest for the trees.

Freedom senses my readiness to begin our canter, but I pause to listen to my body, to honor myself and my body so that I can feel what it wants. In doing so, I feel I am ready and excited to continue our journey and discovery through the forest.

I squeeze my inside leg against Freedom and swing my outside leg back slightly to ask Freedom for the first stride in our canter.

Sweeping through the forest, relaxed and with unbridled enthusiasm, my senses grow to the surroundings of nature. I am free to express myself on this journey through life, yet deeply grounded as I am fully aware of my body and how it is always participating every step of the way.

My excitement grows. This is the life I deserve within the ongoing stream of existence.

As we continue to canter through the forest, I gain a deeper sense of awareness that this state of being is my norm and that life itself is a series of ups and downs, with challenges that only have the potential to sway us and knock us off our center or create a loss of ground.

The wisdom of the body retains the intended memories to instill safety, strength, balance, and deep grounding so that we may easily gain access whenever we momentarily lose any of these.

When we continually practice returning to this natural state of equilibrium, we can return much faster and enjoy the amazing things life has to offer.

This state of equilibrium is the basis for our empowerment.

My ride unfolds with much ease and grace as I feel the waves of confidence that flow through my body and the freedom of doing what I love most.

Animals are the essence of unconditional love, and they teach me that nothing is more fulfilling than opening our hearts to what and whom we love the most.

Traversing the trails, I begin to see that although I may ride
the same trails again, the environment and weather conditions
change and therefore paint a new experience and perspective for
me to embrace.

Yesterday brought rain, the element of water, but today brings sunshine to show me that life is ever-changing, and the more I surrender to the flux, the more I honor the change and realize the beauty life has to offer.

Turning the corner to leave the trail, I transition from a canter to a walk, maintaining my balance and feeling the completeness of the ride with Freedom. I approach the stable with deep gratitude.

Life has its own way of showing us that if we surrender to the moment and embrace it with much confidence, we can live a happy and healthy life by being in this flow.

I feel mutual respect and admiration as I dismount Freedom. I embrace him with a gentle, loving touch, thanking him for sharing yet another day to help me on my way. I share some treats with him and groom him as I did when we started our day together. I realize how much he taught me about self-care in a balanced energy exchange. I wish him much restoration and relaxation after our ride and share with him how much I love him.

My anticipation and excitement build for tomorrow as I look forward to yet another adventure with Freedom. At the same time, if I am to retain a deeper knowing and embodiment, it is important for me to focus fully on my experiences in this moment and all moments as they unfold.

This is the key to mindfulness as it creates the power for me to enjoy the deepest experiences and rewards that stem from my full presence.

Other books by Douglas Macauley

*I Am a Feeling Body: Body Awareness
and Mindfulness for Children
I Am Grounded: A Path to Stability and Feeling Safe
I Am Centered: Finding Your Point of Presence*

Printed in the United States
by Baker & Taylor Publisher Services